Poetry with a Purpose

IN SEARCH OF PEACE

Edited by

Steve Twelvetree

First published in Great Britain in 2000 by
TRIUMPH HOUSE
Remus House,
Coltsfoot Drive,
Peterborough, PE2 9JX
Telephone (01733) 898102

All Rights Reserved

Copyright Contributors 2000

HB ISBN 1 86161 822 0
SB ISBN 1 86161 827 1

FOREWORD

Many people desire peace on earth yet anger and war still continue to this day. People should learn to appreciate more, the wonders of what we have and the gift of our lives and world we live in. It seems that nothing was learnt after the many wars throughout history and in many places people are still struggling for a better world.

In Search Of Peace is a collection of unique poems focusing on people's hopes and aspirations for a united peace whilst taking time to reflect on the beauty of what we already have. Reflections on violence in all its malevolent forms are given along with suggestions on how together we can make the world a better place.

This anthology is a hope for things to come and a celebration of what we have today. Read on for an informative and inspirational look at a better world.

Steve Twelvetree
Editor

CONTENTS

National Secrets	Hugh S McKay	1
War-Free	Marian Curtis Jones	2
To Grasp At Shadows	Molly Rodgers	3
Our Future Needs God's Help	Marion Staddon	4
Conflict	Mary Traynor	5
Broken Wings	Jacqueline Claire Davies	6
When!	Sue Goodman	7
Forever Peace	Celia Law	8
He Is Our Peace	Ken Price	9
Conscience Of The World	Katrina M Anderson	10
Seeing The Light	A Boddison	11
Peaceful Prayers To Say	John Amsden	12
Do Not Harass	Pauline Edwards	13
Learn From Women	Linda Lawrence	14
The Commoner's House	Ray Lewis	15
Violence Forgotten	Betty Green	16
Thoughts Of Peace	E Kathleen Jones	17
A Tribute To The Children Of Kosovo And Chechnya	Vera Ewers	18
A Cry For Help	William D Watt	19
War-Free Eternity	Pat Isiorho	20
Another Balmy Night	David Watson	21
What Price Peace	F L Brain	22
Peace	T M Webster	24
Snapshots	Sue Garnett	25
Disarm! Disarm!	Dan Pugh	26
Ambitions	Jenny Bosworth	27
Which Side?	Susanne Södergren	28
'Hear Him!'	R Gaveston-Knight	29
Light In Our World	Monica Gibson	30
Chiselled Guns	Marylène Walker	31
A War-Time Prayer	Mary Hunt	32
Stop, Look And Listen	Kathleen Speed	33
Britannia	Sheila Waller	34
Think Of God's Peace	Christine Shurey	35
Peace	Ann Copland	36

One Fine Day	G J Reid	37
The Challenge	Diane Simpson	38
Till Christ Comes	Rita Hillier	39
Killing	John Reeve	40
Peace In Ireland	Jean Hendrie	41
A Perfect World	A Whyte	42
Peace	John Rae Walker	43
The World Today	M Wakefield	44
Supporters - No Hooligans	Susan Askew	45
Christmas Peace?	Cathy Mearman	46
The Cease-Fire	Finnan Boyle	47
For Freedom	Beryl Horwood	48
World Peace	Kathleen McBurney	49
Our Work In A War-Torn World	Muriel I Tate	50
Man	Anne Macleod	51
Dove	Alan Pow	52
Peace Of A Dove	Sarah Judge	53
Peace	Joan Williams	54
One Day	Marc Tyler	55
Voice Of An Angel	Audra Ann Murphy	56
Maybe Next Year	Maureen Arnold	57
Peace So Great	Denise Shaw	58
Words Are Powerful Weapons	S Mullinger	59
The First Day Of Peace	Pamela Constantine	60
United Peace And Tranquility	Mary Shaw-Taylor	61
Words Of Comfort	Michael Swain	62
My Hopes And Dreams	Grace Laws	63
Peace	Stephen Gyles	64
Poppies	Jez Scott	65
Eternal Conflict	Christopher Head	66
Profile	S M Thompson	67
Judgement Day	G V Lewis	68
War Game	John Merritt	70
Prospects	Hywel Davies	71
The Good Friday Agreement	D J Price	72
Fighters	Michael A Leonard	73
Xmas	David Richards	74
God Created Light	Uvedale Tristram	75

Disillusion	Dennis Roberts	76
It's Up To You	Eda Singleton	77
The Old Soldier	J E Yeardye	78
Splintered Reflections	Suzanne Stratful	79
Eyes	Amanda Hillbeck	80
Where Have We Gone Wrong?	Jean Tennent Mitchell	81
A Peaceful World	Margaret Upson	82
Oops!	Yvonne Fraser	83
It's Time	Matthew L Burns	84
Glory, Spread Your Wings	Steve Kettlewell	85
Restore Peace	Edith F Adams	86
Medieval Man	J E Royle	87
Peace For The Future	Gillian Morrisey	88
Tears	Helga Dharmpaul	89
Words Of Hope!	Kim Wright	90
Peace At Home	Richard Reddell	91
A Prayer For The World	Melanie M Burgess	92
Grant Me Peace	Carole Revell	93
Still Closer	Elma Heath	94
The Love Has Gone	Keith L Powell	95
50 Years On	Terry Daley	96
Peace In Our Time	Joyce E Williams	98
Peace On Earth	S Brown	99
Dawn Of Peace	Barbara Kern	100
Spirit Of Life	Rossana De Matteis Pinto	101
You Are Near	Nicky Young	102
Peace	Diana Momber	104
A Better World	Kathleen Cleworth	105
Endless War	Chris Blowman	106
Glorious Peace	Alma Montgomery Frank	107
A Russian Tale	Linda Zulaica	108
Top Dog	Jean Paisley	109
Orient Express - A Special Day	Denny	110
The Future	Roy Hedgcock	111
Have Faith	Jim Sargant	112
Every One Of Us	Jeanette Gaffney	114
Peace On Earth	Hannah Cummins	115
All Things Are Beautiful	Arnold R Williams	116

The Return	Patricia Lawrence	117
Ban The Bomb	Peter Steele	118
Peace	Mary Crickmore	120
The Topography Of Ireland	Pam Redmond	121
Parnassus (A Divine Step)	Len Fox	122
Everyone's Tomorrow	Antony Hay Parsons	123
Peace For The Future	Betty Hilton	124
Boundaries Drawn	Paul Darby	125
Freedom For The People	Carolyn Dixon	126
The World Around Us	Jill Booker	127
And From Silence Violence Spreads . . .	Kevin Maguire	128
Reckoning	Mark Morris	129
Great Is The Harvest	Joan Smyth	130
Kosovo 1999	A Smith	121
The Fall Of An Empire	Jill Brown	132
Millennium Peace	J W Holmes	133
Wings	Dennis Whittaker	134
Peace In The Modern World	Kim Darwell	135
Retreat Forward	Robert D Shooter	136
I Saw Jesus	Peter Kuck	137
Desires For Peace	Mahmooda Begum Ali	138
Peace For The Future?	Mavis Simpson	139
Travelling	N Lemel	140
Friendship	Anne McTavish	141
Peace In Our Time	Jean C Pease	142
Desire For Peace	A Odger	143
Lift Up Your Hearts	Blanche Naughton	144
Tranquil Talk	Ruth Daviat	145
The Empty Bowls	J J Mattsea	146
White Dove	Elizabeth Cowley-Guscott	147
Cold	Jordan Steer	148
The Trauma Of War	R Humphrey	149
Abused Symbol	Di Bagshawe	150

NATIONAL SECRETS

Trembling at the thought of war
A nation holds its breath
Yes, it's that old dinosaur
With its contented death.

Injuries, fatalities, destruction
A nation gasps its last
Fired in an eruption
Of an error in the past.

Forgive and forget are treasures
Well hidden from the foe
And peace is just a pleasure
That we will never know.

Hugh S McKay

WAR-FREE

Slumbering dreams of world peace seem so real -
Undisturbed happiness gladness and joy;
All laws respected and work done with zeal -
Good public order no crime to annoy.

Powerful forces united and bold
Combat all conflict by air, land and sea,
Landscape enriched by serene autumn's gold,
Wondrous in splendour glows proud and war-free.

Hope springs eternal for righteous case won -
For justice and truth to one day prevail
When nations agree to ban bomb and gun -
All uprisings quell and peaceful moves hail.

Wakeful awareness of real world uncouth -
Peace of mind, comfort, we find in *God's* truth.

Marian Curtis Jones

TO GRASP AT SHADOWS

We thought, the people who like me -
- Had known their share of bitter war -
- That peace had been achieved, to free
The ones who'd suffered much before!
A forlorn hope - empty it seems
When nightmares triumph over dreams.

Although peacemakers try to grasp
Elusive shadows of the hate -
- That tears so many lives apart,
They often have to watch, and wait,
With each sad day so many killed
The blood of innocents there spilled.

Can we not find a little light
To penetrate that blank, dark wall?
A glow of hope through the bleak night -
- Something of beauty, to recall -
- Those far off times of love and peace.
Will all this hatred never cease.

Molly Rodgers

OUR FUTURE NEEDS GOD'S HELP

Our future needs help
People are going all their own way,
We need togetherness
And God on our side - I pray.

Wars and wars and mighty rage
Murders and crime bring suffering and pain,
Our future needs peace
And God's blessing again.

Drugs and drink so evil within
Bingo and gambling should go,
Our future needs
To come closer to God - 'I know.'

Cancer, AIDS, many people's health is bad
Our future needs God so much,
We need miracles
We need to feel God's touch.

All I can say is what I believe
Get God in our future time ahead,
He is the only help
Before someone presses that button
And no future then - as all will be dead.

Marion Staddon

Conflict

What is this thing called conflict?
born out of selfishness and greed
whereby men who want more power
will cause havoc, to succeed.
Generals and politicians, want to have command
and the innocent are dying
as they defend some peace of land.
There is always some dictator,
wants a bit more than his share.
So he tries to take another's land
with tactics so unfair.
When the conflict's over and the wicked deed's been done
Widows grieve their husbands.
Mothers grieve their son.
There are children without fathers, no one else can ease the pain
Or take the fear from their hearts,
That it may all begin again.
Why can't they put their weapons down, let all the fighting cease?
Then gather round a table
And agree to lasting peace.

Mary Traynor

BROKEN WINGS

All you who are troubled
and living in fear,
keep your faith in the Saviour,
For *He* is near.

Although it may seem
He is gone far away,
He really does hear you,
Whenever you pray.

Man on this earth will have no sway,
Come the glorious Judgement Day.

We will have peace forever
No violence, no pain,
With broken wings,
Birds will fly once again.

Jacqueline Claire Davies

WHEN!

When we can visit Israel and feel there is peace
When we can travel to Ireland and the bombings will cease.
When we can have democratic elections and no one is hurt
When we can see Third World children with food and a shirt
When we can leave our little ones to play without fear
When we can watch television without shedding a tear
When we can feel proud of the football fans when we win or lose
When we can see there's no violence brought on by the booze.
When we can live without fear of road rage and drugs
When we can feel free from crime, hooligans and thugs.
Then we will feel that some justice's been done
And our children's children will know peace has been won.

Sue Goodman

FOREVER PEACE

So once again the bombing began
Putting fear into innocent man
Debris all around where children ran
Nail bombs planted in a car or a van
Designed to maim whoever they can
Mainly those of an ethnic clan

They are ordered out by the end of the year
Putting each and everyone's life in fear
But this is their home, most were born here
And here they should stay this is clear
This death and destruction will bring many a tear
As families lose loved ones held so dear

Who are these people? Who do they think they are?
They can't speak for us all, for many don't wish to mar
Nor do we wish to kill or to injure or scar
It's the like of these we wish to send afar
Preferably in a rocket not a bus or a car
Or sent out to sea in a bottle or a jar

On the twenty-forth of April this bomb in Brick Lane
Just could have caused me personal pain
Because my grandson walked past it down Brick Lane
We don't wish to live where only terror should reign
With small-minded people with a pea for a brain
We should strive for peace, forever to remain.

Celia Law

HE IS OUR PEACE

He is our peace.

He, who has made the two -
one.

Tearing down the dividing wall -
He joins us together -

The stranger,
the alien,
the enemy,
the lover.

Hostility banished
by His love -
sacrifice.

Ken Price

CONSCIENCE OF THE WORLD

What did you do,
What did you say
When they came
To take them away?
Did you try to help them
Or better to stay still?
You might be the next one
That they will kill.
Where was your courage,
Where had it gone,
And will you have more
From now on?
Or will you stay silent
Not saying a word,
Watching poor innocents
Like a flock of lambs and sheep,
Taken to be slaughtered
Because they dared to speak,
When they saw injustice
And hurt and pain,
Wanting a better world
For all to share in again.

Katrina M Anderson

SEEING THE LIGHT

When men shall learn, all nature stands
At the doorway to heaven, or hell on their hands
So shall they decide by virtue or might
To cover the world with ashes, or will it be light?
We all must decide to run or to stay
Upholding the right, let peace have its way.
Deciding is now, as leaves turn to red,
The glow in the sky, or nations fed.
Hallow the ground, the trees and the hedge,
Forgive us O Father, for turning them grey
They wither with poison, let God have His say.
Leaders gather to construct or delay,
I know what I want, the fields all as green,
As pastures with food celestial, or is it a dream?
No, we can deliver, the ever receding scene
When men and women bathe in Bethsada's cool waters.
And lions will lie down, without a scream.
The lamb's in its fold, all is serene
Crops can grow strong, so the soil is pure
Harvests abundant, we can eat for sure
Happiness throngs, as right is outpoured,
Garners are full, hearts are implored,
To fight for the right, to see the light,
So then, our sight is restored.

A Boddison

PEACEFUL PRAYERS TO SAY

Peaceful times
We think will forever stay
But others unseen
But not so far away
Will such faith betray

We cannot pray
For their uncertain hand to withstay
Or the grievous warnings if known
To withstand the bloody revenge
Of those in malcontent alone
Atonement for killing where all conscience flown.

We cannot say
Thus from which deep root
Actions on realms or the life within them
Can flower while we are mute
And animals too do cower. We are not that astute.

John Amsden

DO NOT HARASS

Do not pick on people on other races
You'd be a stranger in their place
Remember we all have our rights
They do too - not to be slighted.

Do not laugh at disabled folk
They're human too as well
Do not laugh at them in their wheelchairs
You wouldn't like to have their cares.

Think before you mock someone's size
Is it really pleasant or wise?
Don't pull a fast one about advancing years
Old folk can be helpful and ally fears.

Picking on the opposite sex
Can land you in a serious check
It could mean police or the sack
Is dismissal worth it what you lack?

Harassers are grown-up versions of bullies
Who pick on work mates and give them worries
Like the bully it meets the same end
No hope, no job, no friends.

Pauline Edwards

LEARN FROM WOMEN

If men would learn from women
What a safe place our world would be,
For we succour, nurture and protect,
It's there for all to see.
With a few rare exceptions,
Women do their best
To nourish, nurse and cherish
Mankind from east to west.
I've met some kind and caring men
So I know they do exist,
They stand out from all the others
Who communicate with fists.
They don't rape, rob or rampage,
They are caring, loving and kind,
If all men were more like women,
Humanity could bind.

Linda Lawrence

THE COMMONER'S HOUSE

Posturing politicians
  And militant MPs
Belligerently bickering
  Quite openly on TV.
All of our chieftains
  Never agreeing to agree,
The quaint, the queer, the quarrelsome
  Are left in charge of you and me,
Many sit most silently
  Slumbering in their seats,
Only elbowed into alertness
  If there's an Opposition Bill to defeat,
Accusations fly alarmingly
  Boos and jeers is how they greet,
'Order, order,' screams the lady
  Trying desperately to diffuse the heat.
Yet, there is one time of harmony,
  All you will hear is resounding 'Ayes,'
It's when you are broke and desperate
  And they vote themselves a payrise.

Ray Lewis

VIOLENCE FORGOTTEN

It puzzles me to hear that violence does still erupt,
And that all folk can be so very abrupt.
Could it be that many don't know the meaning of peace?
And therefore can't understand when they hear that all
Conflicts should cease.

It does appear that the worse they are - the more they have,
Why is it some folk can't behave?
Is it because no example is set
Or does the juvenile think that it doesn't matter yet?

Do young people not think how bad they make things for all,
And that they could be the sufferers in their fall?
They may then rue their wayward ways,
And wish they had listened in earlier days.

Betty Green

THOUGHTS OF PEACE

How dreadful the outlook for victims of war and strife,
What have they to look forward to in their future life,
Homes destroyed, loved ones killed or dreadfully maimed,
And the evil perpetrators, not one bit sorry or ashamed.

Sad, orphaned children looking puzzled and lost,
Bombing having ceased, but at what a cost,
Nothing left but ruins and complete desolation,
Facing homelessness and maybe slow starvation.

Can't something be done to bring wars to an end,
So many people's future on this depend,
Talking things through to make enmities cease,
Helping to bring about an everlasting peace.

Maybe the culprits could be threatened to bear,
All the atrocities they have made others share,
Would that bring about a change of mind and heart,
Could it be ideas from which to make a start?

If the sale of arms could be banned from countries at war,
Maybe hostilities would cease and peace reign once more,
What a wonderful world in which to live,
Able to relax and a peaceful future to everyone give.

Having no more fear of destruction and pain,
Expecting past terrible events to recur again,
Everyone, all enjoying life, not having to worry about tomorrow,
With peace assured, leaving behind tears and sorrow.

E Kathleen Jones

A Tribute To The Children Of Kosovo And Chechnya

Lead them into the light Lord,
Those blessed mites, maimed for life,
Let us all take them to our hearts,
Away from affliction and strife,

Injury in any form puts fear in a child,
Yet these children from afar suffered more,
Blindness and disturbed minds,
Such happy souls long before

As another tragedy unfolds in this sad country,
We should count our blessings one by one,
We can only be with them in spirit,
And in our prayers as each day is done,

Take them in your arms Lord,
Let them know we care,
May their broken spirits be healed in time
Lord in your mercy, hear our prayer.

Vera Ewers

A Cry For Help

The spiders spin their webs of deceit
With the ants ordering their soldiers to meet
The killer bees that can strike at will
And the bloodthirsty lion that likes his fill,
This world of ours can be so alarming
With blood and gore that's never charming
We tend to forget the poor and needy
With a child cry out '*Mum* please feed me.'
We think of ourselves and what we can gain
And never remember the people in pain
To change our world would take time to come
But Hey! There is always the next millennium.

William D Watt

WAR-FREE ETERNITY

Schooled in visual technology of our age
We cease to see the writing on the page,
While static of our time blocks our listening
And we cannot hear the word
That makes for inner or outer peace.
There is no space for our voices to be heard
For the speedometer of life has us breathing
Beginning and end in the same breath,
And we can know no living without fear
Of nuclear death.
Let us snap in half the plastic pen that signs
Away liberty of men,
Turn out the light of self-justification that blinds them
To their own hypocrisy,
Let the currency of our new age be peace
Given in love and returned with freedom.
Come dream with me for I have a dream to dream
As I sleep floating the stream to a war-free eternity.

Pat Isiorho

ANOTHER BALMY NIGHT

As sanity fades away with the setting sun
Swarms of hooded figures engulf the streets
Gathering like wolves to bay their intolerance.

Petrol bombs arc an ebony sky
Before cascading at random on parked cars
Heralding the start of another balmy night.

Stark dancing flames highlight naked violence
Truncheon and shield lash out, brick and stick return fire
As the vehicles of law and disorder collide head on.

Acrid smoke assaults both perpetrator and peacemaker
Cacophonous inane sounds echo and vibrate
Encircling this once peaceful neighbourhood.

Patel's electrics, Murphy's music, common sense now charred ash
While hatred and sweat congeal on street corners
Eyeing discarded booty strewn on violated pavements.

Saneness returns with the sun's first rays
The post-mortem and clean-up begins
In this suburb of Saravejo or English suburbia.

Community pillars have crumbled in bewilderment
Their stillborn words fall like snowflakes
Only to melt away in the hot, morning sun.

An ill-directed bloody brick thrown by a misguided hand
Stands as a lonely sentinel in a demolished doorway
Of a sheltered housing complex.

Now only the rancid smell of fear lingers
As a nightmare momento to another barmy night.

David Watson

What Price Peace

So much effort has gone forth to get peace
Between people and nations on earth.
Papers are signed and promises are made
Often not kept and the writing not worth.

Enforcing rules and compromise is not the answer here
We need to understand the cause and the reason for hate and fear.
All have a right to viewpoints but not to thinking they're right
For all have different opinions and some are ready to fight.

For a cause in many countries
is something that's right and true.
Nothing will change their viewpoint
whatever you say or do.

On the surface peace seems uncertain
As nations seek for power.
And rulers govern ruthlessly
As they gaze from their ivory towers.

Scripture speaks of peacemakers
A role that is hard to fill.
Trying to fathom another's mind
And helping a stubborn will.

This may not solve great issues
But prayer can change all things.
For God understands the cause
And He can a miracle bring.

Our part may be humble but needful
As we pray for those who seek.
For a peaceful solution to world affairs
That strength may be theirs, though weak.

So God give them wisdom and guidance
Whatever the problem or land.
May they give Thee all the glory
And be led by Thy mighty hand.

F L Brain

PEACE

Late lark sings from quiet skies
and from the west, sun
his work done
lingers in contentment
falling on grey city
luminous, serene
a shining peace.

Smoky haze descends
rose-clad light, spires
glow, change. In combe
shadows rise; lark sings on
sun chasing benediction,
sinks. Curtain closes.
Train of stars
decorates her cloak.

Gift-sheep passing
long day is done
quiet hush waves on shore
lark fades away
in my heart is peace.

T M Webster

SNAPSHOTS

As the Century's circle turns,
I see men walk on the moon.
While on Earth, many walk homeless.
Looking down the years, I see millions
Squandered on war and weapons,
While many thousands die of hunger.
In the New Millennium I see a vast wasteful Dome,
While in Africa, men drown on treetops, waiting for aid
Inadequate and slow to arrive.
As the New Millennium dawns, I see
Champagne and fireworks, love and laughter.
Resolutions for a better World.
Please . . . let it be.

Sue Garnett

DISARM! DISARM!

We have long since outgrown the need to kill -
Our brother's blood to spill
Or to do him harm.

The crude creations of a crude age -
When men killed in unabated rage -
Are long outmoded.

This farm called Earth
Will grow and flourish
If we will turn our skill -
Reinforced by will -
To ending war's alarm.

Disarm the world and let all Mankind rise
To shun violence when disputes arise.

When nations disarm
All thought of war will cease,
And ample wealth
Come to our hands
To spend on health and housing,
Water and good food
For all Humanity.

Banish thoughts of war -
Disarm! Disarm!
And there will soon arise
A new race,
With Love shining in their eyes!

Disarm! Disarm!
Let bloody wars all cease -
Then shall our children's children live in peace!

Dan Pugh

AMBITIONS

Let's have an ambition.
There will be peace throughout the world
The people of Kosova go back to their homes
Without a bomb hurled.

Let's have an ambition
That no one breaks the law.
Burglaries and muggings a thing of the past
Things we all deplore.

I know it will never happen
A dream that will not come true.
But I'll try not to do horrible things
And I hope the same goes for you.

Jenny Bosworth

WHICH SIDE?

Swords clashing all around,
you must decide;
> which side?

In this life or death struggle
can truth, love or
righteousness win?
Or have deceit, hatred,
destruction
gained yet more influence?

A serious fight,
about you,
your own personal life,
truth,
history
and restoration -
the world you live in.

The battle hard
the outcome uncertain.
Put on your armour,
now!
And decide;
> which side?

Susanne Södergren

'HEAR HIM!'

Filled with Grace and Truth . . . how sad . . .
What lovely attributes He had,
This matchless Son of God most high,
This paschal Lamb so soon to die . . .!
And have we seen Him face to face
And felt the ardour of that Grace,
That power which shone within His youth . . .
The very idyll of pure Truth . . .?

Come Christian, great rewards are here,
For to believe brings lasting cheer,
We may take hold in faith and stand
As princes in a barren land . . .!
And witness of what we can see,
Incarnate Son of God is He
Who grants us heirship, bids us love,
As there . . . the Spirit settled like a dove
Upon His gentle, glorious Head . . .
'Hear Him . . .' the voice of God had said.

R Gaveston-Knight

LIGHT IN OUR WORLD

The world of today needs positive thought,
To bring about change for our good.
We can transmute every negative thought,
If we use unconditional love.

Some countries we know have much darkness
The light has just vanished away.
Each heart has a light to shine out in the dark,
Please use it, don't throw it away.

The golden age, soon will be dawning.
When 'Peace' everywhere will then reign.
It's hard I agree to image . . . but -
'Light' will have triumphed again.

The world has increased its vibration,
And we're spinning fast you'll agree.
Think 'gentle' thoughts friends, not violence.
'Thoughts Live', and they touch you and me.

Monica Gibson

CHISELLED GUNS

Withered soldiers on bleeding grasses.
Forgetfulness in their pockets
Steams with remnants of sweat.
Their boots are manacled to the field.

Mother tends an empty cradle
Her womb robbed of rebellion
In her eternally inaudible sobs
Level with mud and torn affection.

When peace lays all guns to rest
Like ragdolls in great big cots
Fathers will chisel wooden ones
As Christmas presents for their sons.

Marylène Walker

A War-Time Prayer

Dear God, if we ask for bread, will You give us a stone?
If we cry through the weary night, will You leave us alone?
Shall we beat our hands for a thousand years on a brazen pitiless sky?
When we pray and suffer and weep, will you leave us alone to die?
No! Though our hearts be black as the night which we in our
                                           folly made;
Though our souls be dead as Your holy peace which low in the dust
                                           is laid;
Though our sins be red as the brother's blood which to Heaven for
                                           vengeance cried -
You will turn again and bring us to life, the people for whom You died.

Mary Hunt

STOP, LOOK AND LISTEN

The angel bowed down her head
As she gazed upon a thousand dead,
The end had come too soon, this she understood
For those who lay in pools of blood,
A teardrop ran down her cheek
As she waited to collect the remaining weak.

She knew it was not God's will or God's way,
It was man who chose this judgement day,
When they took up arms and went to war,
When they could not find the words anymore,
The value of their principles escalated in cost
As friends, families and generations were lost.

The reasons why it began will be forgotten tomorrow
As each act of violence becomes a revenge for sorrow,
New tactical moves are planned without shame
And the difference between life and death is a game,
The highest of intelligence becomes deaf, dumb and blind
And sensible solutions create a confusion of minds.

Peace will come when mistakes have been rectified
And the hunger of anger stops gnawing away inside,
When bridges are built and barriers are brought down,
When we all understand that we share a common ground,
That our survival does not depend on another's sacrifice
And that there's nothing wrong with simply being 'nice'.

Kathleen Speed

BRITANNIA

Britain used to be the best
Now we are mixed up with the rest.
With the EEC I don't agree
I am British and always will be.
Decimalisation was bad enough
But money all the same - it's insane.
There will be no point in going abroad
Lose the novelty of foreign currency.
Doors are open to Tom, Dick and Harry
And be let in just to marry.
Many visitors stay and not return
Give state-aid that was not earned.
Britain is best we used to say
Until our values went astray.
Before plastic goods, foreign labels
No more local grocer.
They have been taken over
Mum and Dad fought for Britain.
Will it now be in vain?
Britain has all it needs
Without joining the EEC.

Sheila Waller

THINK OF GOD'S PEACE

As I look round the world
Today I can't find peace,
But wars and fighting, bloody men.
They grip so hard and never give in,
Making men and wives, small children too
Lives a misery, no food, no clothes, shelter,
O shame you men of war, listen carefully,
It doesn't take much to love our fellow man,
Give up your guns and weapons of war,
Think of peace, what you could give.
Because Jesus opened his arms and died
For one and all that's true love of God.

Christine Shurey

Peace

It was so peaceful by the lake
With just the sound of the tufted drake.
So quiet by the still, clear waters
Wasn't expecting any squatters.
But I know him so well
With his little tuft so swell.
Often camouflaged by long reeds
Paddling along, sometimes at great speeds.
But I'm not blind
Taking off there like the Golden Hind.
The Spanish Armada trying to defeat
Sailing along without your fleet
Just like Sir Francis Drake
To the waters and off you take.

Ann Copland

ONE FINE DAY

One fine day there will be no wars
People would settle disputes
In an arbitrary way
With a councillor or referee
From each political faction.

No winners, losers, especially no dead
Nor tears of hatred, bitterness shed
With every man, woman, child walking home
To an easy, sleep-filled bed.

Then laughter and joy
May permeate this lush, green earth
Even your favourite God might drop in
Just to shake some hands;
Declare, 'Now you are mankind.'

G J Reid

The Challenge

What does it mean
To be free and alive?
What can you do
To live and survive?

Dangers lurking everywhere
As Mother Nature can be so cruel
Accidents, hurricanes and earthquakes
Why cannot men live by her rules?

Nuclear weapons and CS Gas
Why did man invent these?
Is he not happy with material things
He is too greedy and does as he pleases!

The world alone, will destroy herself
Where man will no longer thrive
Ask again, what does it mean
To be free and alive?

Diane Simpson

TILL CHRIST COMES

We pray for peace,
But there is not any,
In this world,
Till Christ comes,
In prayer, we pray that the spirit will come,
Come to live, in everyone,
Till Christ comes again,
Never knowing, where or when,
Christ will come.

All the signs that we see,
In the world around us,
Foretold in the Bible,
These things must come.
Before the world is 'Free'
When Christ comes again.

Let us pray for change,
In ourselves,
For only then, can Christ come,
Changes start, with you and me,
Before we can change the world,
Till Christ comes.

Rita Hillier

KILLING

A flock of starving starlings
Descend upon a field of worms
Worming their ascent for breath
From beneath water-logged fields,
Feed full and then fly on.

The lioness stalks a single, weaker quadruped,
Kills, and her and her family feed sufficient, then sleep,
Whilst hyenas and vultures gladly take second pick,
Before saphrophites clean Nature's plate quite clean.

The creatures of the sea swallow each other,
Size by size in turn like an infinity of annular tubing;
Even so, only sufficient for thriving.

Such are God-created perpetuation patterns -
But the creature with the most scheming brain of all -
His creation, war, the most senseless killing of all!

John Reeve

PEACE IN IRELAND

Will the trouble, in Ireland,
Ever be solved?
Will there ever be harmony,
With the two sides, involved?

For there's plenty, of talking,
But it's a mystery, to me,
Why they can't, just shake hands,
And promise, they'll both agree.

So I hope, when an agreement, is finally reached,
Men who have children, and wives,
Can be friends, with their neighbours,
And all lead, peaceful lives.

Jean Hendrie

A Perfect World

Dreaming of the future
Perfect in every way
No more corruptions
Or children led astray.
No more homeless
Getting into drugs
Or old people
Being mugged.
No more murders
Wars or bombs
No more violence
Or broken homes.
A peaceful future
Free of sin
Everywhere bright
And clean within.
If this dream of
Mine unfurled
Then we would have
A Perfect World.

A Whyte

PEACE

Truth appears now and then
After applause it bows out again.

Patience waits at the end of the queue
It counts to ten to itself staying true.

Anger boils after simmering for a while
And then explodes without rhythm or style.

Love caresses so gentle and kind
So happy with perfection, in heart and mind.

And peace gives all by taking everything away
It sweetens and restores come what may.

John Rae Walker

THE WORLD TODAY

Sad world! full of trouble, hate and war,
Have you forever on peace closed the door.
Is man determined to live in strife . . .
To waste the precious gift of life.
Values are scattered far and wide,
By succumbing to selfish pride.
Can you not see where this will lead?
Are you too blind to take heed?
From experiences past which have taught you nought,
Through all the wars which have been fought.
Yet still you make the same mistakes,
And will have to learn,
However long it takes.

The innocent suffer, the children and aged,
While those in power rant and rage.
Like 'Chess Board' pieces wrong moves are made,
And man is a pawn in the game that is played.
The prize if power, but at what cost?
Is love and fellowship forever lost?
As the mind of man becomes more enlightened,
The 'not so learned' are very frightened,
Of what lies ahead in the years to come.
For the younger generation who have to go on,
For what will they see as their guiding light?
Will their lives too be one long fight.
The power of thought is very strong,
And a united world will never come.
Until you learn to think aright,
The world will always be in this plight.

M Wakefield

SUPPORTERS - NO HOOLIGANS

I went to France on one of the ferries
Saw English hooligans who were merry.
They went to France to watch England play
Most of them ended up being locked away.

Fighting broke out, people cut, stabbed or maimed
Lay in hospital, never to watch the football game.
Where is it leading to, what's it all for,
Is football becoming an eyesore, a bore?

When so-called 'supporters' spoil it for others
Degrading our country, our fellow brothers.
Then this is the time to stop being aloft
Stand back and weight up the damage, the cost.

Put them in prison, don't give them a fine
That's like giving a child one hundred lines.
Hard labour wouldn't be too cruel
Let's get back to the game of football.

Susan Askew

CHRISTMAS PEACE?

If Christmas is the season of peace and goodwill,
Why do we still see violence every day
In our newspapers and on TV?
Why do wars and conflicts never end?
As soon as one battle is resolved
Another conflict starts up somewhere in the world.

What a terrible mess we have made
Of this world God came to save!
It must be breaking His heart to see
What mankind has done to spoil the earth.

Come again, Dove of Peace, to heal our land,
Restore our peace once more.
You alone can bring order out of chaos
And peace instead of war.

Cathy Mearman

The Cease-Fire

The announcement of the cease-fire
Heralded the end of the political pyre.
All those wasted lives
All those widowed wives.
The burning emblems of faded pity
Shell-shocked epitaphs of Belfast City.
The orphan boy laments
At promises not kept by history's remnants.
Of twisted allegiances and spilled blood
The primed bomb timer has stopped with a thud.
Ancient echoes of conflict resolution
The gunman seeks absolution.
For nationalism is death's fellow traveller
Revenge - no seeds of hope will gather.
As one approaches the flagrant dawn
One prays for peace - not a flag torn.

Finnan Boyle

FOR FREEDOM

My soldier boy, he marched away
My soldier boy, he could not stay.
He went to fight for freedom's right
For freedom's cause he was trained to fight.

He look so proud and felt so brave
As the underdog he went to save.
He was so eager to right the wrong
To aid the weak, for he was strong.

He's not strong now, my solder boy
No longer filled with laughter and joy.
He's shattered since the landmine struck
Seems my soldier boy just ran out of luck.

I love him so, he clasps my hand
And tries to remove my wedding band.
I'll never leave him, come what may
How I wish he'd never marched away!

Beryl Horwood

WORLD PEACE

The years roll on since world wars gone,
And the message is still the same,
All war is futile, no one can win,
We had to fight back to save kith and kin.

We say we want a better world,
For all children to inherit peace,
We can help this to happen if we really believe,
The world owes all children a lifetime received.

Our priorities hold our children's future,
By the example we give to them,
There's a need to build on the goodwill to all men,
Lest we forget, wars can kill us and them.

We should know by now what really matters,
Greed and hatred will never find peace,
God's wonderful creation is for all to share,
World-wide prayer is the life-line to God who cares.

Kathleen McBurney

OUR WORK IN A WAR-TORN WORLD

When Jesus asked Andrew to follow Him
Andrew soon brought his brother as well
And that's the best way for us all to work
If Christ's gospel, to the world, we're to tell.
For it's Christ's command that we speak and we show
His peace and His saving grace.
So, to every person we need to give the good news
Sharing His love, in this honourable race
That is the way that the world can be saved
And rid of its dark war-torn spots.
They're all caused, as Christ Himself well knows
By the scourge of sin's selfish blots.
Strife follows sin and more sin follows strife
And that is the way the 'world' goes.
This vicious circle needs to be broken for sure
But how to do it? - only Christ knows.
If we bring folk to Him, He will teach each His plan
As in their lives He entwines His own peace.
Then, if each will obey, God's plan can become whole
And conflict, from that moment, will cease.

Muriel I Tate

MAN

Time waits for no man
Time
To bring peace
Time
Man will venture into the unknown
Time
May it bring peace
Peace we ask of you the One above
Let us go forward in time
With peace and love.

Anne Macleod

DOVE

Let's release,
A dove of peace,
As it travels from coast to coast,
Spreading word of Holy Ghost,
Across the seas,
Steered by the stars,
Promising an end to wars,
As it travels from East to West,
On a distant sand,
It comes to rest,
There a poor native cups it in his hand,
As only he can understand,
Its message of love,
And so this simple savage,
Who knows nothing of war's ravage,
Sends it on its way with a gentle shove,
Bon Voyage my wondrous bird,
Travel on to where peace is just a word,
A word no one has ever heard,
And where tranquility's absurd,
Go on take flight,
Travel by day and night,
Till mankind gives up his fight,
And peace is ours by right,
The chance is slim,
The chance is slight,
For brother to turn to brother,
And simply love another.
So journey on,
The voyage is long,
And so's the quest,
And so the dove finally must rest.

Alan Pow

PEACE OF A DOVE

A dove flew through
My window, and said to me
'Peace will come with
Love and tranquility.'
I asked the dove
'How could this be?
With countries at war
And people fighting
Even more.'
He turned to the window
And said to me,
'Always believe
In the power
Of your dreams.'

Sarah Judge

PEACE

The world, they say, is full of crime,
Will we ever see peace, in our time?
Through the deeds of sinful man,
We live our lives, as best we can.
God sent his Son, the world to save,
For our sin, His life He gave.
We go to church and we pray,
Please, Lord, give us peace today.

Joan Williams

ONE DAY

One day;
All peoples from
All nations
Will live in
Peace and harmony,
Without
Hatred for skin;
Or religious divide.

One day;
Maybe not tomorrow,
We can call
Our fellow man
Brother,
And together
Share the wonders that
This world provides.

And one day;
The hatred we see
Will be a thing
Of the past,
And all peoples
From all nations
Will stand
Side by side.

Marc Tyler

VOICE OF AN ANGEL

Not a missile fired, a gunshot heard,
tears of continued laughter
now takes pride.

No rage of anger, unsheltered hate,
joy and compassion
who said it's too late!

No hooligans roam, violence on streets,
peace in communities
Heart of friendship beats.

No play is unsafe, shadows in the dark,
hand of compassion
Is never too far.

No scream unheard, a cry ignored,
comfort at hand
Rich or poor.

No words of war, faith ever jibed,
spirits awoken
Honesty without lies.

>Is it an empty dream we see
or is it a reality fate will be?
That blue skies will hover
no clouds of doubt,
for the next generation
we leave beauty and love.

Audra Ann Murphy

MAYBE NEXT YEAR

If only there could be,
Peace in the world, for you and me,
People living together, side by side,
Nothing to fear, nothing to hide.
No traumas or tragedy,
Is that too much to ask, for you
and me.

No senseless killing all living in peace,
living in harmony, hostilities could cease,
No more wasted years,
Or shedding heartbroken tears,
Maybe in the new century,
This will happen, for you and me.

Maureen Arnold

PEACE SO GREAT

A time of darkness reigned this Earth as total blackness came
Agreement would not be seen, for ruination was the aim.
And yet within this machine of evil being
Peace would come, peace for seeing.

In totalitarian warfare which meant to rule this Earth so grand.
Would be seen an evil hand.
Atrocities never known before
With depravity at their core.

Yet in all of this we saw the hand of God
Is that not odd?
People in their hearts rejoice
Broked a resistant voice.

And so when peace came to the world
Those people had their hearts unfurled.
In themselves they found their peace
A peace so great that it would never cease.

It will never take away the crime
And neither will the essence of time.
But this peace gave strength through this hideous storm
They no longer find the need to perform.

Denise Shaw

WORDS ARE POWERFUL WEAPONS

I hate all forms of violence,
And in fighting I see no sense.
Debating can decide an issue,
Arguments are trouble for you.
Words may be our strongest weapons,
Are catalysts which spark actions.
Speeches can provide us with peace,
Words, truces are reached using these.

S Mullinger

THE FIRST DAY OF PEACE

Gently the day must come
To the world of Traders' Town,
Like a cloud of snow-white birds
Softly floating down,
Each feathering a nest
In the hardened mortal heart,
Warming the buried core
Where peace again can start.

So that, one shining morn
When the sun comes out to play,
People will run to people
With gifts to give away:
Forgiveness of misdemeanours
And all the slights that irk,
The wish for new beginnings
And the will to make it work,

Till we are a sharing people
And everybody loves
And we are the human embodiment
Of those symbolic doves.

Pamela Constantine

UNITED PEACE AND TRANQUILITY

United peace and tranquility is what I'm hoping for,
So please open up your hearts and pray to the Lord.
As in the Bible, the Lord Jesus said, 'We are all brothers,'
And so all over the world, we need to help one another.

There's Famine, Floods, Earthquakes,
Fire, Landmines and Killing,
Violence, Rape, Abuse, Illness,
And help if all are willing.
    Willing to understand,
    Peace and tranquility,
That most of us have in our homes.

And to see the joy of happy families,
Good food, clothes and smiling faces,
Let our hearts go out to all! The
Unfortunates, in different Races.
We are all here today reading our poetry,
Giving joy to each other,
This is United Peace, and Tranquility,
And yes! We here are all family.

So it's up to all of us now, to put things right,
To bring back United Peace, and take a look,
At love, as love is Peace and Tranquility,
Like the two Beautiful White Doves,
So let us pray in our hearts, for all this
    To our dear Lord up above.

Mary Shaw-Taylor

WORDS OF COMFORT

To live in peace
Is everyone's wish.
It will not be easy,
With troubles that exist.

But only by trying
To fight and achieve
Freedom for all
In an idealistic weave.

Start out fresh
With new ideals and dreams.
Spread the word peace,
In magnetic streams.

Unite as brothers
End conflict and pain.
Let's restore peace
Long lasting, to remain.

Families and friends
Can help play their role.
So that we all
May reach our goal.

Which is peace in our land
To stay and remain
As our Father in heaven
Surveys all our domain.

Michael Swain

MY HOPES AND DREAMS

My hopes and dreams,
Are all in my head,
There's more than there seems,
While I think of more in my bed.

I wish for the world safe,
Or to have robots, that's what I mean,
What about something new,
Which has never been seen.

I know just the thing,
Cures for horrible things like cancer,
That's what I wish,
And to see Santa's reindeers like
Rudolph and Dancer.

My hopes and dreams is to never harm animals,
And don't even hurt one fish,
If you want the world like this,
It'll be one millennium wish!

Grace Laws (8)

PEACE

Find a quiet place
far from the bloody chaos
of a world in conflict . . .
clear your mind and contemplate
to enable you to gain
the power to help
the desperate people
suffering the brutality
of a merciless warring world.

Now you can transform
their fear-filled lives
as they are regenerated
to become a powerful living force
which will bring a lasting peace
to a new serene and caring world
as the evil weapons of war
are destroyed for evermore.

Wars have afflicted mankind
since man first appeared
upon our spinning globe
but now permanent peace
will spread tranquility
with wisdom and justice
upon a sad war-weary planet
and this will be
a revelation for humankind
as a new age is born to earth.

Stephen Gyles

POPPIES

See the history of Verdun,
Shot skulls of the First World War.
714,000 killed and wounded,
Maybe even more.

Thousands upon thousands were not buried,
But rotted where they lay
Amidst the wounded who died from gangrene
In the stench of death and decay.

As the days turned warmer
Death choked the breath of the air.
The earth was ravaged with corpses,
Rotting corpses everywhere.

Turn the pages to the bloodbath
Of the Battle of the Somme.
1,265,000 men
Dead and gone.

In the holocaust of the trenches,
Pure hell of its stench and pain,
There isn't a word for this horror,
It doesn't possess a name.

Nothing but soldiers dying,
All dying for the cause
Of the First World War,
The war to end all wars.

To be remembered with poppies.

Jez Scott

ETERNAL CONFLICT

The troubles all around the world today
Revolve around the greed for power to rule,
To subjugate, to have the final say.

Religion is one reason for dispute;
Convenient excuse to 'fight for right'
And agitate, while peace-lovers stay mute.

The colour of the skin gives cause for strife;
Superiority of one to other
Is false, for God grants all an equal life.

The tribe and language often start great rows
'Twixt adversaries, proud of heritage;
Unwilling to review their tribal vows.

The ethnic claim, 'Originally we
Lived here, and you came after', means that you
Are simply, in their eyes, a refugee.

Another world-wide conflict has this source:
Minorities well armed and loud of voice,
Intent to rule majorities by force.

How easy it can be to itemize
The causes of the conflicts in the world;
How difficult to find some compromise.

So long as life exists, there'll still be greed
To fuel the strife, and we must struggle on
To put out fires, wherever there's the need.

Christopher Head

PROFILE

Pro-American in all cases of conflict
Splashing around the Pacific Ocean
Mind how you climb
You may fall down slowly.

Pro-American in all matters political
Search out the culprits ready to go
Where your heart takes you
A picture on the mantlepiece typical.

Pro-American in all areas of culture
Gone out to live there briefly
Encounter those who feel the same
Profile on an Irish writer.

Seems to be alright on the night
Recollections of the beauty queen
Play Italian be there at my waking
Beauty queen just seventeen.

Only seventeen a dancing queen
Which girl looks like Abba
You are a special lady
Midnight folly, Cinderella.

Beauty queen poses for the paparazzi
Was it a joke guest of Italy
Close to the Greek coast
Beauty queen, pretty woman.

Married to Turkish Airlines
Smoke pollutes the air
Windows open door ajar
Bounced back with a question
Where will you go 'Lady'
Why Sir, where the heart takes me.

S M Thompson

JUDGEMENT DAY

The Saviour of the world came in to land, trailing no clouds of glory from his Oxford brogues, or his pin-striped suit, he carried a smart briefcase in his hand instead of an olive branch, but peace came with him, and stayed forever.

His silver eyes saw man's violent powers as sicknesses of the mind that needed the answer he alone could give: in desert hills he built beacon towers of strange unearthly metal that sang in the wind, and seemed to shimmer.

He measured all the patterns of mankind, calibrating those feelings of greed, hate and fear; that drove them to war, then with loving hands he tuned his strange alien machines to send a signal round all the Earth.

In a playground a boy struck his brother, and fell; his own face bleeding: the other untouched by the aiming hand.

As children flinched from a raging mother she dropped to her knees screaming; her ears still ringing from her own cruel blow.

A husband's hand left his young wife unscathed, but, his own jaw was broken, and fear filled his mind at this swift judgement.

All around the world the weak or enslaved cringed from the expected blow that never landed, yet felled the bully.

Now, all wars were just useless heroics;
even in a long range war the attacker died when his own bombs fell.

Drug pushers writhed more with each sold fix, and died: one for each OD, till there was none left throughout the whole Earth.

The robbers and thieves found their fingers burned and left their booty lying where they had touched it, and this crime ended.

So every individual's crime was turned; aimed straight back at their own heart, or mind, or body, and in time; they learned.

With no one's mind or body degraded; gentleness bred gentleness, and love reflected doubled in strength: The ages rolled past. The beacon faded; starved of reflected evil; its work completed; it crumbled to dust.

G V Lewis

WAR GAME

They said 'It's only play!'
and made me hide with blackened face
in the still of winter's night.
To crouch and ache in dampened hay
in a cold and cheerless place
with little appetite to stand and fight,
but a hunger for tomorrow's light of day.
They said 'It's just a game!'
And when the dawn came in at last
and shone its ray of warmth upon my grimy skin,
I recalled my country's military past
and why her foes had tried to disavow her might.
I knew my number, rank and name
and why, at last I came to fight.

And they said, 'It's just a game!'

But how should I feel, if this were real?
Would I go with gall enhanced
and sharpened bayonet fixed,
with my brothers to advance
betwixt splintered tree and foulest trench,
until the stench of broken bodies
made me near to faint?
Would I fear the sight that would surely
taint my wounded soul
for me to sit and paint this wretched scene
of rotting wood and stinking hole,
and bloody death at seventeen?
Would I forget my number, rank and name,
or, worst still, forget what I had seen?

And they said, 'It's just a game!'

John Merritt

PROSPECTS

Amid the murky miasma of modern life
Where violence, famine and pestilence are rife,
Prevailing philosophy is 'I'm alright, Jack,
As others do to you, do the same to them back.'
Killing has now become a long-distance affair,
Efficiently expert, certain, performed with flair.
An artillery barrage can soon be laid down
Targeting precisely an army or a town.
Bombs can be dropped from heights beyond the naked eye,
Raining down without warning from a clear, blue sky
On to designated targets, postage stamp size,
The bombers heedless, not hearing the victims' cries.
Many experts are worried Earth's population
Will quickly increase to cause much tribulation,
For they aver the power of the world to feed
Humankind is limited, will not meet man's need.
What then to this dilemma is the solution?
Curbing through proliferation of pollution?
Active destruction by violence, famine, war,
Anarchic behaviour, abandonment of law?
The world population could rapidly decrease
Though no one could possibly guarantee the peace,
Even the continuation of human life
Once deadly chemicals and bacteria were rife.
Does the possible destruction of humankind
Damage our faith in the perfect goodness of God?
We should remember it may not be in God's mind
That all men can continue where their fathers trod.
God's Word speaks of Armageddon, the last battle,
Which precedes the final destruction of the Earth.
If we believe this as truth, mankind's death rattle
Is our future, and women will no more give birth.

Hywel Davies

THE GOOD FRIDAY AGREEMENT

The Good Friday Agreement
   Was a very special one.
Folk asked, on the announcement,
   'Has a miracle been done?
All the bitterness and conflict,
   Are they really now to cease
With better days in prospect,
   In a true and lasting peace?'
That Good Friday Agreement
   Was arranged by mortal man
And therefore is imperfect,
   Very different from God's plan.
From prison came releases
   Of some guilty of great crimes,
Whose wicked, evil actions
   Brought much horror to past times.
How many, in repentance,
   Seek forgiveness from above,
Turn round and follow Jesus
   On the better path of love?
A Good Friday Agreement
   Would be better news, for sure,
If people came together
   At the Cross, to Christ adore.
That newsflash would be glorious,
   Then hostility could end,
The Prince of Peace victorious,
   Known by one and all as 'Friend'.

D J Price

FIGHTERS

Men of the regiments were sent to fight
Against others with children and wives
Defending a cause so making it right
To kill other men and take their lives

Although surrounded by skin and bone
Of fallen comrades and enemies alike
The warriors fought their battles alone
Stepping over bodies left in the dyke

Victory is sweet, bathing in glory
Returning home with spoils of war
All through the ages the same story
But within man himself lies the flaw.

Michael A Leonard

XMAS

A child will look forward to this day
        in hopes of new toys and games to play,
house adorned with trimmings and holly
        family and friends all making jolly.

With food in abundance, the meal is set
        we gorge ourselves silly, and yet,
no thoughts are spared for those in need
        who beg and grovel, hungry mouths to feed.

Third World countries upon this Earth
        pay dearly for food, the price is death,
while sat by the fire, Xmas cards being read
        spare a thought this year, for the Third World dead.

David Richards

GOD CREATED LIGHT

Come cease this talk of war and sing
For we can find old pleasures still
In shattered worlds and still can bring
Light hearts to see the sunset hill.

For still the murmuring river runs,
Mocking our dark with its myriad mirror'd suns.
The stars that with bright reflection chide
The waiting world with light, our fear will hide.

Though feet are groping in the towns
Where valour hides away her crowns,
Yet beauty dims no torch for fear
But kindles brands and throws a flaming spear.

If we to be so seen court death
No star nor moon will darkened be;
Their life is light and light is heaven's breath
That fills the air for man to see.

Let darkness tease the shrunken street
And steal our days with curfew knells
And subtly trip our homing feet
Yet beauty flaunts abroad and rings her bells.

Let clouds' cold bars shut out a star
Then sudden moon will break the sky
And curious visions float afar
Where white birds wing and fly.

Ah man, poor man must have such sweet deceit
For God Himself created light
No war nor murder's crazed conceit
Can wrest its beauty from our sight.

Uvedale Tristram

DISILLUSION

You sit so cosy
You feel so warm.
While outdoors
Blows the raging storm.

In days gone by
Wars were fought.
They said, for freedom,
Was it worth nought?

We still have worries.
We still have strife.
People still take
Each other's life.

Your home is safe.
Your walls stand firm
And you wonder if people
Will ever learn.

Dennis Roberts

IT'S UP TO YOU

Peace starts with a smile
Mother Teresa told us so,
We should listen and learn
And use our brains,
Try not to be selfish and vain
For life is too short and we have
Such a lot to gain.
We are all here for a reason
Black, white, yellow or brown
To share with each other the places
From which we came.
And when we go, we should leave
A little glow so that the next
Generation will gladly follow.
Life is a glorious gift to be
Enjoyed not destroyed!
So let us make friends and
Tie the loose ends.
We are here on loan, nothing
Is our own
Make peace not war and
Enjoy the rapport
Peace starts with a Smile.

Eda Singleton

THE OLD SOLDIER

In a darkened room, his thoughts profound,
An old man sat, deep armchair bound,
Gazing long into the depths of a flick'ring fire,
His mind returned to painful memories, dire,
There he sat, forlorn, biting hard on his pipe-stem,
And felt himself reborn, once more, to war mayhem.

Then, as nations called proud men to war,
And his mind recoiled from the heavy guns' roar,
At the going down of the sun, he remembered them,
The bright young men, the years would not condemn,
But they would never rise again, to plead their case,
To rail and shout, in vain, for others of their race.

Where then, the dignity, the innate grace of man,
His lonely dreams of home comforts shattered?
To fight and die for England, entrapped in the ghastly plan,
Bold illusions of grandeur long since scattered!
Only a thick, muddy trench for *his* mortal remains,
To cover the stench of his woebegone pains!

The old soldier, no angry tears would allow,
To dim his mem'ry of the field of valour,
Had answered the call, had kept his vow
To his companions at arms, resting in bloodless pallor,
To keep his yearly vigil, sad thoughts in his breast,
As he stood on a lonely hill, with the bravest and best.

Proudly bearing their battle scars, they found eternal rest,
Brutalised, traumatised, fallen comrades, lost to the world,
Had prayed, 'Let tomorrow's young men be spared the test,
Let today, the guns stay silent, their shells unhurl'd,'
Their message shall be told; the old soldier had not fought alone,
For none shall grow old, each brave spirit, to God had flown.

J E Yeardye

SPLINTERED REFLECTIONS

The shards of original Paradise
Smash, broken, stabbing and fallen to Earth
Transform what could have been to no surprise -
A living Hell: splinters bleeding and death!

Ingenuity is raped in terrorism:
Young children hurt; born to blood baptism.
So, if God is good, brave, tell it to them!

Livid we lived, Devil cursing our praise;
Praying for peace yet fighting for pieces of land!
Blood-soaked fertility rite
Striving with heart and begging soul for right
To raise not raze
A host of angels
Not a horde that mangles.

Choke on incense in the sense
That innocence
Is destroyed: Hell, drowning anti-matter
Yet it matters
As warring blood splatters
Starved, skeletal bone clatters.
Such a massacre - why did the mess occur?

Not for God the serpent's sly whispers,
The mad dog and fear stroking through his fur,
And not for God the blazing sword at Eden.
Men are vermin, rats reflecting star
While Satan sounds like Saturn
And Jupiter was once called Jehovah
But the choice is only man's decision!

Suzanne Stratful

Eyes

Look into my eyes, what do they say?
Can you see the story of their life?
Can you read between the lines?
See the picture that explains it all?
The lack of colour and the heartache.
The love they need, the love they've lost.
All the love they've given.
All the love they need to take.
Look deep as you can and try
to read the pictures they have painted,
over years of pain and frustration.
The words no one can say.
The action no one can give.
Read the eyes and see the hell they are in,
and the heaven they wish for.
The fire they burn and the fragrance of
the flowers they long for.

Can you love these eyes that are so desperate to care for?
Can you show them the path that leads the way?

Amanda Hillbeck

WHERE HAVE WE GONE WRONG?

Can't even get a seat in the park
vandals destroy them in the dark
Can't enjoy the newly-planted tree
vandals snap them in half just for a spree

Deface what they can, score cars with knives
slash tyres, rip spoilers, not very nice
God only knows when will it change
I know myself I'm partly to blame

Indulging our children - by not saying 'No'
The whole picture we just cannot see
For taking the easier, softer way
it's now society has to pay

True what they say we reap what we sow
a shame for the good kids, nowhere to go
Not even safe to go to a dance
vandals there - so they're taking a chance

So much drink and drugs on the scene
out of their heads, don't know where they've been
Until the next day when all unfolds
they only remember by being told

A passing phase - I don't think so
it's us as parents - which way to go
Leave it in the hands of God
destroy our morals - 'No,' he said . . .

Jean Tennent Mitchell

A Peaceful World

A peaceful world as God meant it to be,
Our children growing up to be free.
We do all try to fight for peace,
But our efforts seems to be on the decrease.

Violence continues in many lands,
All because some have disagreeing plans.
They don't want peace for the future,
They take all like a hungry vulture.

We know what has happened before,
But our children don't need another war.
People homeless, a lot were killed,
Their lives were never really fulfilled.

Are we reaching out into the dark?
Where is the dove that left the ark?
For us all, God opened many a door,
He gave us bread to help the poor.

So now let all be at peace,
And let conflictions start to cease.
A peaceful world, we won't have to pretend,
When all the violence comes to an end.

Margaret Upson

Oops!

They strayed along the wrong road too far,
In the wrong, they stole a posh car.
Into the fast lane they did strive,
Through town and country fast they did drive.
No consideration was their care,
As to the open road they did share.
Abruptly came to a halt as they came to a crash,
Stopped with a mighty bang and smash.
'Oh God, look what we have done,
No more joyriding, all the fun's gone.'
Now they have to go home at policeman's will,
To be roared and shouted at. Parents ready to kill.
Yes, they've made a big enough mistake,
Never! A stolen car again will they take.

Yvonne Fraser

IT'S TIME

Through the everlasting sunlight,
In my private land of dreams,
Flows a stream of truth and kindness,
Filled with happy golden gleams,
In every little ripple there,
New wisdom is unfurled,
And oh so clear in an eddy here,
Is the freedom of the world,
I see great bonds of friendship,
The mighty oceans span,
And instead of constant war,
The brotherhood of man,
There hasn't been a soldier yet,
Who didn't ask, 'In war,
What recognition will I get,
What am I fighting for?'
To keep from being fired upon,
He has to kill or maim,
In fact, he's just a helpless pawn,
In a politician's game,
You'll never see a war brought on,
By ordinary folk,
It's time for common-sense to dawn,
It's time the masses spoke.

Matthew L Burns

GLORY, SPREAD YOUR WINGS

Glory spread your wings thus wide,
Across pastures and green hills high,
Obeisance flow with love in accord,
Then redemption shall linger nigh,
Sing doves of peace to foretell such joy,
To all nature and mankind the same,
Then upon Earth shall dwell such peace,
Through the Redeemer's holy name.

Glory spread your wings today,
And bless our descending night,
So stars in unison with paradise shine,
As the moon portrays a divinity bright,
Upon the new morning spread afar,
Such purity for eternity to last,
Amid the sunshine above pastures grand,
Grant solace and unity be fast.

Glory spread your wings worldwide,
So understanding shall reside again.
Then liken to Eden's unmolested land,
Wide honour and grace shall reign,
With faith and trust in Jesu's name,
All sins would emerge long past,
Then man could live for evermore,
With brotherhood and love to last.

Amen.

Steve Kettlewell

RESTORE PEACE

Let us look inside ourselves.
Do we see Truth. Compassion. Contentment,
Or sadly, only flaws?
Yes. The flaws are there.
Man still craves the Forbidden.
Though fearful of this craving
He lacks the courage to deny it.

Unlike the beasts of the field
Who only fulfil their needs,
Who know neither avarice nor sloth,
Who nurture and guide their young
In the survival of their kind,
Man reigns supreme unto himself,
Blind to another's worth.

Blind to values of innocence.
Blind to the essence of joy.
Loath to step aside
To let another be first.

Man owns an exquisite world.
Owns fertile fields and sparkling springs.
Owns protective trees, has foods from the seas,
The smallest insects are Man's servants,
Their work balances nature
To nourish and honour Man eternally.

Now! Let us look outside!
Acknowledge those unsought gifts,
Those which are the tools for Peace
Which awaits Man's reverence,
Which awaits Man's husbandry.
Only thus, can Peace prevail.

Edith F Adams

MEDIEVAL MAN

A thunderous crash, a brilliant light
streaked across the darkened night
Medieval man could not understand
why such a bright light was in command
for this humble person if you think back
a brain with intelligence he did lack.
Many moons ago and before man had any idea
anything out of the ordinary he did fear
A stranger came amongst them, so it is said
did He work miracles with fishes and bread?
He was considered different, people didn't understand
He spread His words all over the land.
They say He had a halo or was it a helmet?
He could cure the sick from city to hamlet.
So if He was so good why did He have to die?
Yet three days later He appeared to fly.
Medieval man still does not understand
that this so-called man was from this land
for when they entombed Him in silk and lace
they did not consider this man was from outer space.
So the believers built their shrines and places of worship
and still donated coins and gifts even in hardship.
But man has developed and is so sophisticated
they will worship their gods and are so dedicated
they even had guidelines and many a law
but they do not talk, they would rather war
Medieval man has changed in a quite different way
Religious leaders should get together and have one say
then maybe the death of the stranger will not be in vain
Medieval man could live in peace and with a lot less pain.

J E Royle

PEACE FOR THE FUTURE

Third World people starve to death
While there's food and provisions in the west
Countries fighting countries
In the name of religion and greed
Oh Lord, whenever will there be peace?

Old people mugged for savings
In their homes or on the streets
Some children have met a violent end
Simply by playing out with friends
Violence seems everywhere, oh when will it cease?
Will I in my lifetime ever see peace?

My hope for the future, a world full of peace
When all wars and conflicts will come to an end
Food for the hungry, the homeless found homes
Man seeing man, not as enemy but friend
Our children growing up in a society
That is carefree and safe.

Gillian Morrisey

TEARS

Crying, Father, I'm crying.
All around me Your creations are dying.
Your special children, we humans, keep killing.
We look and we talk and seem willing
To do better - but only tomorrow.
I am filled with pain, shame and sorrow.

Here we are, Father, killing our brothers,
Our fathers, sisters, and our mothers.
All life around us, we are hurting, destroying.
Interruptions we find annoying.
Never happy, unless we are breaking
All, that Your love has once been making.

       Is this, Lord, what *free will* is all about?

You did not teach us hatred, yet in Your name
Many have killed and are killing again.
With blood they put out love's eternal flame.
Calling to others: hate! kill! and maim!

Ev'ry tear I cry shouts: 'Enough is enough!'
Father, dear Father, in heaven above
Send once again the Pentecostal dove
To fill our hearts with compassion and love,
With Your peace and Your love.

Helga Dharmpaul

WORDS OF HOPE!

If you've ever survived through conflict
Or lived in a war zone
I can't imagine how you felt
I can only guess it was alone.
Take these words
Carry them inside
Wherever you go however lonely
Someone is always by your side.
Have faith in the good
Trust it to be there
No matter how hard it gets
Someone out there will always care.
Be strong and never waiver
Even when you think you can't cope
Read this statement
These words of hope.

Kim Wright

PEACE AT HOME

Lord Jesus, bring us peace,
Amongst our families, and friends:
In Your grace, please release
Your Love, in us, to mend
Divisions in thought, word and deed -
That we would not cease, to plead
The cause, of those that are near.

Lord Jesus: all power in Your hands -
In Your mercy, release the bands
That shackle our hearts,
From seeing the best
In those that we know:
Please, let Thy Spirit flow -
That each one of us, starts
To invest
Your Love.

      Amen.

Richard Reddell

A Prayer For The World

Let there be love in the world and not hate
Let there be peace in the world and not war
Let there be hope in the world and not despair
Let there be plenty in the world and not hunger
Let there be generosity in the world and not greed
Let there be help in the world and not want
Let there be harmony in the world and not discord
Let us all pull together in this world forever.

Melanie M Burgess

GRANT ME PEACE

God grant me peace and serenity
in this world of chaos and strife.
Help me to find the Christ within,
to uphold me throughout this life.

Help those in war-torn countries
to find the strength to go on.
Help us all to realise that
peace can't be fought for nor won.

For peace is a quality of the soul.
It's at the very heart of creation,
and God grants this peace to all
who seek to lift this world's vibrations.

So let us nurture our planet
Help war and pollution to cease.
Let it start with me, Lord.
Grant me Your loving peace.

Carole Revell

STILL CLOSER

Though situations now worldwide
Appear as chaos without hope,
We won't despair. Our God is closer still,
And sovereign is His power, supreme in scope.

The future so unknown can cause
Vague fears and seething thoughts which scare;
But close - between alarms ahead and me -
Is Christ my Saviour, always hearing prayer.

So very close are troubles which
Affect my body and my health.
But even here my Saviour's closer still
For He's within, imparting spiritual wealth.

Elma Heath

THE LOVE HAS GONE

The love has gone but here the look stays on
As the photographer takes his shot
For about this family he knows not a lot
On this, a wedding day.

The love has gone but here the look stays on
As they photograph a family gathering
In many ears bad news that morning really is still ringing
As they all gather together.

The love has gone but here the look stays on
Right until the very end
When one of the family lives no more
My, oh my, what can be in store?

Keith L Powell

50 Years On

Today we look back fifty years
and celebrate those years of peace
through many eyes filled with tears
and many prayers for wars to cease.

We see again those massive crowds
outside the palace awaiting
some singing, some cheering out loud
events of long ago reliving.

Mixed emotions, joy and sadness
come flooding back for us today
a time of laughter and of gladness
deep memories in every way.

Fifty years of peace we've had
but somewhere there's always fighting
but no world conflict has occurred
some measure for celebrating.

Programmes remind us of yesteryears
then see us as we are again
Times of anxiety filled with fears
some with laughter and some with pain.

Harsh times remembered by the old
rationing and deprivation
blitzes and bombs so I am told
Deeds of bravery and duty done.

Celebrate the freedom for all
many peoples in many lands
remember those who had to fall
while you listen to the marching bands.

See the bonfires and signals blaze
hear the speeches from one and all
wonder in the eyes of people's gaze
for generations to recall.

Terry Daley

PEACE IN OUR TIME

Think of peace instead of war
No more hatred anymore
Think of flowers instead of guns
Let there be harmony for everyone
Why don't we just think of love
And just be kind to everyone?
No more heartache, no more pain
Do let peace forever remain
It's not so very hard to do
Just let a little kindness through
Then smile and just say you care
A helping hand and time to share
Do a kind thing every day
When times are hard, just kneel and pray
For the more you hate, the more you will
It's just like swallowing life's bitter pill
In the end it will eat you away
And for ever and ever that's how you'll stay
Unhappy with life you'll stay as you are
There will be no happy day or no shining star
So why not change your life right now
And if you really don't know how
Fill your life with thoughts of love
Look and pray, to God above
And in the end love will remain
Then you will be at peace again.

Joyce E Williams

Peace On Earth

The world in which we live, it used to be a wondrous place,
But mankind has destroyed our Earth and left it in disgrace.
The trees and plants were plentiful and everything was green.
We robbed her of her luscious growth and slowly swept her clean.
The oceans and the seas were once so clean and blue and pure.
We fed to them our poisonous waste and made them one big sewer.
The air was once so clean and clear and free for us to breathe.
We filled it with our toxic gas, pollution and disease.
But not content with killing off our precious Mother Earth,
We then turned on each other and the roles have been reversed.
The violence of our race has brought destruction and despair.
The death and mutilation of our kind is everywhere.
We wage war on each other as we did with our good Earth.
We kill and maim and torture and for what is it all worth?
When will we learn our lesson, when will the fighting cease?
I wonder will we see again, a world that's full of peace.

S Brown

DAWN OF PEACE

Will there be an end to war
In time that is yet to be
When people love each other
For all the world to see

When man has learned his lesson
And wants to live in peace
And all the hatred and the greed
Has started thus to cease

The innocent no longer suffer
And leaders are not bad
And we walk towards Utopia
In lives that are not sad

Man can reach the highest state
Or descend down to the low
But with God's blessing from above
The good will start to show.

Barbara Kern

SPIRIT OF LIFE

Silent perfecting dreams
Surrounded by exquisite beauty
To create a world with no fear
With longing for peace and harmony

Wisdom of life
Flower of grace
A wondrous mystery in
The sea of space

To touch the stars
And have the key
To ride a rainbow
Into infinity

To dance the waves
With the rhythm of the ocean
Setting the spirit of life free.

Rossana De Matteis Pinto

YOU ARE NEAR

When the sun is shining in the sky,
and the air around is very clear.
When all the birds sing as they fly,
then I know You are ever near.
When children joyfully do play,
and people all turn to smile.
I know that this is a happy day,
You are with us all the while.
Flowers are in bloom and leaves are green,
the wind whispering in the trees.
When all of God's nature looks serene,
I hear You calling me in the breeze.
You created these things with such great love,
for all creatures, both great and small.
Intending Your world to be as Heaven above,
with Your love surrounding us all.
Surely my Lord, You must shed a tear,
as the wars rage and people fight.
When Your people forget that You're even here,
surrounding them with Your wondrous sight.
One day Your world will be the place,
You meant it to be from the start.
When all will behold Your glorious face,
and Your world with love will impart.
Once that day comes, You'll cry no more,
My Saviour and my Lord.
Your face will still smile and Your glory outpour,
on Your people whom You've always adored.
Meanwhile my Lord and Saviour so dear,
some of us love You and know,
we're with You in love, aware that You're here.
Alive to the glory and love You bestow.

I hope You find comfort my Lord so divine,
in these words that came from my soul.
The deep love I give You in every line,
is to help You to fill this great hole.

Nicky Young

PEACE

The sun is shining on the summer hills,
Warm ocean breezes touch the flower-starred land.
The peace of heaven is here on sea and sand,
Dark cliffs, green valleys, silver sparkling rills.

Peace breathes across the restless world again;
Of Earth be stilled, as are the waves, the sky;
Be open to the love that cannot die;
The unseen healer of all hurt and pain,
Who, at long last, brings once feared death, to be
A birth more wonderful than the sun's light;
Than skies of stars transforming darkest night:
Release of souls into eternity.

Diana Momber

A Better World

Let us all try that bit harder,
To make the world a better place.
Give a helping hand, whenever we can,
Wipe a tear from some sad face.

Why not give a smile to a stranger,
It wouldn't be hard to do,
And be assured that stranger
Would smile right back at you.

A little touch of kindness,
Would go a long, long way
To some lonely person
Who has no one to share their day.

Let's try to do something worthwhile,
No matter how big, or how small,
Just helping a neighbour along the way,
Or answering when they call.

To know there is someone near you,
When you are most in need.
A friend who will share your burden,
Is really a friend indeed.

Just say a little prayer each day,
That you will always do what is right.
God is there, and ready to listen,
For we are precious in His sight.

Kathleen Cleworth

ENDLESS WAR

Shattered ruins all around what was once our beautiful town.
Buildings swaying in the breeze, windows shattered as our dreams.
Curtains flapping to and fro, torn and tattered to adorn no more.
Our lives will now never be the same, only sadness still remains.
Loved ones gone, never to return, just the ghosts of yesterday
remain here today.
Too many innocents were lost along the way, for a war that will
last forever or so it might be said, maybe there is hope along
some distant path.
Let us live in harmony as we did before and stop this chaos before
we become the never more.

Chris Blowman

GLORIOUS PEACE

Peace can reign
If the global folk restrain
From searching for their own gain

Life will be good for all
Should the wreckers have a reckoning call
By letting their meanfulness go by the ball

Happiness will then come to stay
The world will be jolly and gay
It will be easy to work that way

Love will reign with the peace
Everyone will be at their ease
I'm longing to see this world at peace.

Alma Montgomery Frank

A Russian Tale

Poor Gorby took a holiday:
Whilst on a beach he sat,
His friend and aide did bring about
a classic coup d'état.
Let's pray it's not too long before
Old Gorby's back in place,
And Russian find its peace without
A messy coup de grâce.

Linda Zulaica

TOP DOG
(A cynic's viewpoint)

The people at the top if they
need a war,
the rest of us all just believe what
they say it is for.

It's easy to lie to people especially
the youth,
Pilate came out straight with it when
he said 'What is truth?'

It should be much harder to brainwash
people now,
but, when you look around they act like
a CJD cow.

We could argue day and night who is
right and wrong,
but, it still suits the richest few
to weed out half the throng.

Until the rich control their greed for
lust and luxury,
they'll goad the poor with nothing to
lose to fight through history.

Jean Paisley

ORIENT EXPRESS - A SPECIAL DAY

An excursion on the Pullman of yesterday
Came to our town to whisk us away.
The jazz band played us off on our trip
As we sat with our champagne taking a sip!
The comfort and ambience of this super train
I long to experience again and again.
The food and the service was second to none,
We lived for a while in an age that's bygone.
The wine it was flowing as through countryside
We sailed on the tracks, a luxury ride,
A magician joined us to entertain
And seemed to throw my jewellery out of the train.
The day was spent in luxurious fun
A good time was had by everyone.
Invited as we were to walk around and see
The pictures in each coach in marquetry,
The brasswear, the furnishings, the sheer luxury,
The Pullman's the best, I'm sure you'd agree!
We were transported away to another time
When all that was offered was surely sublime.
The day seemed to belong to a wonderful age
Where we seemed to be 'at home' centre-stage.
Time slowed down to a leisurely pace
Away from the city, the work and the race.
We were pampered in style and exquisite taste
We quickly forgot the usual haste.
When the excursion was over, home we did go
Calm and relaxed and incredibly slow.
We felt like we'd been away for a while
We all floated home with a light-hearted smile.

Denny

THE FUTURE

Pisces is passing,
the age of Aquarius emerging.
As with mother and babe
labour is painful;
so much to be rooted out,
dispersed, eradicated
to make way for the dawn,
the dawn of brotherhood,
love, compassion.
Blossom cannot turn to flower,
to fruit
if at the root
there is poison.
Be not fearful, apprehensive.
Be thankful for the opportunity,
the chance to participate
in this glorious Birth.
All is good. All is well.
All *will* be well.

Roy Hedgcock

HAVE FAITH

In this world of evil,
anger and pain,
where your sun has set
and won't rise again.

In this world of tears
and shattered dreams,
where the nights are long
and the nightmares scream.

In this world of sadness
and broken hearts,
where your life's lost meaning
and fallen apart,

Have faith, believe,
there will come a day,
when your pain,
will slowly fade away.

It will take time,
it won't be easy,
but open your heart,
help is there, believe me!

I know, I've been there,
lost and alone,
in that great black void,
in that dark unknown.

It seems so simple
to hide away,
but with the dawn
comes a bright new day.

It's there for you,
it was there for me,
so open your heart,
then your eyes, you will see.

Jim Sargant

EVERY ONE OF US

Why can't we all
Try to live in peace
With other *religions*
Their colour of creed?
Every one of us
In our world today
Should love each other
There must be a way
How can you hate
Someone different from you?
They too have feelings
Like me and you
Why should we be
So intolerant of them
Simply because
They don't look the same?
Let us remember our time is now
Let us bring harmony
Back into our World.

Jeanette Gaffney

Peace On Earth

A butterfly's wings surround us all.
The beauty can be seen, obviously.
We unite as one on this Earth
We are nothing but thieves of beauty
We thieve as the night falls
And the sun arises
We have no shame
We harm not only ourselves
But the rest of this pitiful place.
The beauty lies within our hands
Let's keep it safe.

Hannah Cummins

ALL THINGS ARE BEAUTIFUL

All things were beautiful
Perfect was the world of ours
All men, women, pure to God
Amongst the trees and flowers
Beasts of Earth - birds of sky
Now the world was at peace
Nobody was arguing, nobody asking why
Why God made the Heavens
The seas, mountains and the sky?

All things were beautiful
Everyone was happy, everyone did smile
All was to last forever
Not for just a while.

Arnold R Williams

THE RETURN

It thrills me to the marrow
when a robin hops so near,
This to me foretells of future times
when there will be no fear.
The time when wolf and lamb
in harmony will lay,
and by the viper's nest
in trust . . . a child will play.
When He who gives us 'second birth'
returns in triumph to planet Earth.
These things I know will come to be
in the fullness of time for all to see!

Patricia Lawrence

BAN THE BOMB

Time is running out now,
That I understand.
Soon the metal monsters
Will engulf the land.

It is no good running,
Because there's nowhere to go.
There will be no freedom
When the nuclear bombs blow.

I just want to live on.
I don't want to die.
I don't want to sit in awe
As bombs fall from the sky.

We just want to live on.
Can you hear our cries?
We are all just sitting ducks.
Bang, bang, bang! Everyone dies!

Don't believe in nuclear warheads
Because they are our suicide.
Don't believe in chemical warfare
But in the Lord God confide.

Perhaps you think I'm joking,
But inside I know it's true.
Humankind has taken its final curtain,
And mother earth has too!

Peace is now a feeling,
And love is just a word.
The Bible's words of freedom -
Are they ever heard?

I just want to live on
But I don't know why.
I don't want to watch in awe
As millions truly die.

Peter Steele

PEACE

Peace is what we pray for
Month after month, year after year,
So many lives, are uselessly lost,
It is time, that the end of the wars are near.

We are in the year two thousand,
Time to start anew,
Stop all this fighting and killing,
And bring love, and peace into view.

Mary Crickmore

The Topography Of Ireland

Once it was green
this sad grey island full of stones.
Each stone seems to represent a voice
that has cried out for its own kind of freedom
and then been petrified at that impossibility.

All around the island
stones lay side by side,
companions,
as they never were before.
Their differences are lost in their similarities.

When no one is listening do they whisper together
and cry some tears
for the bullets and bombs,
while somewhere the Blarney Stone waits for kisses?

Pam Redmond

PARNASSUS (A DIVINE STEP)

If Jesus were to write a poem
What blessed words He'd say,
He'd speak about the faith that lives
Within this world today.
For He has watched us through the times
Two thousand years in all,
And He has seen how Christians ever
Answer to God's call.

If Jesus were to write a poem
How meaningful the rhyme,
In words of praise He would speak
Of blessed Christian clime.
For everywhere in hymn and prayer
Since first on earth He came,
The faith He handed down to us
Each region speaks the same.

If Jesus were to write a poem
Each verse we'd ever cherish,
For He would say 'til end of time
God's dream would never perish.
He'd tell us how the light of faith
Forever would unite,
All the people of this world
Who keep His love in sight.

So when you take the time to pray
To Him who'll lead us home,
Be inspired by what He'd say
- If Jesus wrote a poem!

Len Fox

EVERYONE'S TOMORROW

The formula for peace, is in our hands.
Whether or not we follow it, depends on us.
How much do we really care, or understand?
It can't be left to others, we hold it now, in trust.

Everyone's tomorrow, starts with today.
So if anything is to be done, for a peaceful future,
Then it needs to be done right away.
There's not a moment to lose, *world* peace to procure.
No time to pick or choose, we mustn't delay,
The longer we leave it, to shake hands with one another,
The harder it will be, to welcome back our brother.

Peace for tomorrow, depends on a cease-fire today.
No compromising the future, with complex conditions!
It must be realised, and accepted, we each have different ways
Of living and worshipping, and following traditions.
All condemnation, must be truly forgotten,
Not stored away, to be recalled in pain.
No accusations, all transgressions forgiven.
Wipe the slate clean, and start again!

The formula for peace is in our hands; do you understand?

Antony Hay Parsons

PEACE FOR THE FUTURE

Will the world never learn to live in peace?
Is fighting and killing never to cease?
The world could be such a wonderful place,
If it wasn't spoilt by the human race.

Two thousand years after Christ's birth,
We still can't live in peace on earth.
Thousands are killed almost every year,
And many more still live in fear.

League of Nations - did not bring peace -
United Nations - wars still did not cease,
What is wrong with the human kind
That killing is all they have in mind?

For heaven's sake can't we find the way,
To live in peace in this present day?
Can't men get together - improve everyone's life,
Can't we please make an end to this pointless strife?

Betty Hilton

BOUNDARIES DRAWN

Whispers, whispers,
Then shot gun blast.
Cracked paint dried in heat,
Of helicopter rage.
Splintered glass,
Smashed on window pane.
Hinged door moving,
Creaking,
In amongst petrol flames,
As dogs whimper, children cry.
Guns fire with distant howls.
Then amongst long grass,
Bullets cut across knees on barren plains.
Shanty towns of the murdered,
And deranged.
Killing fields of charcoal.
Cut horizons, etched by bullets,
And scratched onto the earth.
Nothing left except, to hope, to end,
This tragedy of guns,
On lines drawn.
Boundaries blown apart by senseless blame.
In our fragile cases,
We pray for the voice of reason,
To surface again.

Paul Darby

FREEDOM FOR THE PEOPLE

Why can't the nation of Ireland, go back to the basics of life
Let a woman live with her husband, and their neighbour live
                                        with his wife
Return to how it all began, the way life's meant to be
No words could describe the happiness, if these people could be free
Have separate religions if they must, but respect each other's ways
Accept that there is only one God and it's sure to bring brighter days
God put them all upon His earth, He gave them all free will
He wanted them to prosper, not bomb and shoot to kill
One day they will realise, that the innocent people matter
God will condemn these ringleaders, then the cowards will all scatter
Purgatory awaits these sinful souls, for them it could be too late
The innocent victims will rise above as they wait at heaven's gate
If you love your country and repent of all your sins
Then God will grant forgiveness, then united you will win
Ireland our people are pleading with you, make all this hatred the past
Break down the barricades and become a nation created to last.

Carolyn Dixon

The World Around Us

War, famine, poverty and crime
The inner cities full of grime

Plants, birds, animals and trees
The aroma of blossom on a springtime breeze

Pollution, infections, cancer and smoking
We must not forget the global warming

Music, writing, drama and song
Teaching the children right from wrong

Peace and harmony across the lands
The world around us
Is in *our* hands

Jill Booker

AND FROM SILENCE VIOLENCE SPREADS...

This is a dissonant age,
its sounds symptomatic
of a deeper malaise;
an irritant that swells,
an untamed voice that quells
the sweeter harmonies.
Its beauty, too, lies thin
- no deeper than the skin -
a guise that masks
disfigurement within.
And from silence violence spreads
and enters into empty heads,
loud and crude and rude and coarse,
a crowd - a mob that rules by force,
its noise destroys, like wanton violence,
the peace that only comes from silence.

Kevin Maguire

RECKONING

When the days are all but over
and still your foe stands tall,
then no matter how great your courage
comes a time when all must fall.
When the fight goes on forever
and the battle long and hard,
sometimes even the bravest hand
must hold a losing card.
No matter the unfairness,
disregarding luck and cost,
fate's law moves on relentless
and every chance is lost.
Remember there's no shame in losing
when true you fight your best,
and I pray that the harder the road
means an ever sweeter rest.

Mark Morris

GREAT IS THE HARVEST

Children are dying, but what do *we* care!
They're not in our family - just people out there.

Mothers are searching - often in vain
To provide for their families a handful of grain.

Men in a parched land sowing their seed,
Hope for a harvest to alleviate need.

People in countries divided by war,
Wounded by bullets, disfigured and scarred.

Hindus and Moslems - still unaware
Of God's great salvation - but why should *we* care!

I'll give you the reason we should be concerned.
It's found in the gospel of Matthew, I've learned.

Jesus our Master, who came from above
Set the example of showing God's love.

He had compassion on all whom He met.
Touched them and fed them, so let's not forget.

He expects us to follow the path He has trod
To care for the helpless and point them to God.

Great is the harvest - there's work to be done.
We, who are Christians belong to God's Son

The hungry need feeding, the poor need our help.
The sick need attention - we'll give from our wealth.

Let's wake from our slumber - there's no time to spare
To show God's compassion and *prove* that we care.

Joan Smyth

Kosovo 1999

Women, children and the elderly run out.
No young men can be seen about.
A child stands crying in the road alone.
He's been kicked out, of his only home.

Forced onto the road, in his bare feet.
Thousands like him, ordered onto the street.
Ethnic cleansing, can this really be.
Shown on the world's stage, for all to see.

Now NATO decides to play its part.
In go the stealth's and the bombing does start.
A human train forms, on a track in hell.
Food and water needed, to keep people well.

No place, for them now to call their own
Were they lived, was it only on loan?
Being an Albanian, is not a crime.
Hitler's practical, has come back for a second time.

A Smith

THE FALL OF AN EMPIRE

In two world wars they fought and died,
Young soldiers full of British pride,
They bravely gave their lives that we
Could have a future, safe and free.

Then politicians had their way,
And gave all what we had away.
Politics and union greed
Cut Britain's flesh and watch it bleed.

While precious jobs were thrown aside
As industry collapsed and died.
Productivity hit the board,
And manufacturers moved abroad.

All too soon, it took effect,
No jobs, no money, no self respect.
Social unrest began to climb
With petty theft and violent crime.

Yet, it's a fact quite widely known,
That charity begins at home.
And people's faces say it all,
They've had to watch an Empire fall.

Such a sad and tragic story,
No more the land of hope and glory.
Those long gone soldiers, proud and brave,
Must now be turning in their grave.

Jill Brown

Millennium Peace

So much money has been wasted at this millennium time
Each country trying to outdo the other for no real reason or rhyme
And whilst all this jostling for recognition has been going on
People throughout the world have been dying one by one

Dying because of tyranny, dying because of greed,
Dying because their country had no food on which to feed
And yet, all of this money has been poured down the drain
To impress a small minority who think life is just a game

All countries talk of peace and yet still need to understand
That peace begins *within, at home,* and in *their own* land
Why let people live in squalor right in front of your eyes
Then scream and shout when you see them about and act so surprised

Peace is a contentment, which is felt throughout the land
Peace is something we *all* really need to understand
It's not just thoughts of war or how to beat the rest
Peace is a perfect balance between the worst and the best

As Nations we live in peace and yet within each one no more is done
So now *people*, throughout the world let us heat up like the sun
For we must each become peacemakers, wherever we may be
Then across *all* our lands we may join hands in peaceful harmony.

J W Holmes

WINGS

If we had wings on which to fly
What would we see from way up high
What would we see from high above
Would we see a world of love

Or would we see a world of war
As on wings above we soar
Would we see mankind in need
As on wings above we speed

What can we say, what can we do
Can our wings help me and you
To fly away to a better place
Where there is love for the human race

But as on wings above we fly
It's only then we come to realise
That peace for man and a world of love
Can only come from up above

So the heights we reach with our wings
We come to see we could never bring
What God alone above can do
Bring joy and love for me and you

And so the wings on which we fly
The wings that take us way up high
Will only really help us know
That only God can stop man's woe

Then as we journey on our wings
We come to see that God will bring
A paradise on earth so new
Where we can fly, yes me and you.

Dennis Whittaker

Peace In The Modern World

Peace is a word that exists as only letters
A feeling though, it is never expressed
Prayers are heard but never fulfilled
And tears fall but are never seen
Hatred reigns in masses
Pain and suffering consume the soul
Heartache lives inside those capable of emotion
Corruption, scandal, death
War, famine and destruction
All words that fall on deaf ears
Lived each and every day
Society creates the monsters
That hide behind a slogan and a smile
Power corrupts creating what we see today
Modern society is a joke
Life has never changed
Human nature cannot be undone
Eternally we will live in fear
Below those who dominate in power
War, death and pain are part of life
But those good few make it worth living
Through all the bad exists good
And Heaven is built on this foundation
Life though hard is worth the pain
Heaven awaits those who are good
And the Devil stokes the flames for those who are not.

Kim Darwell

Retreat Forward

Peace just invades
like searing a boil
extracting an aching tooth
eradicating evil
retreating from mammon
an attack of good
writing off debt and poverty
letting Christ's cross win.
If this is not God infiltrating
I would like to know what on earth it is.

Robert D Shooter

I Saw Jesus

'I saw Jesus in Buchenwald,'
The oberlieutnant said.
'Just as we shut the oven door,
I saw the thorns upon his head.'

The GI saw him in Vietnam,
He was in a paddy-field
Just before they napalmed him.
You could tell the way he kneeled,

Was it, Jesus in Alabama
Hanging from a tree?
And when he comes on Judgement day,
What colour will he be?

Is Jesus there in Ulster,
In orange or in green?
Are they too dazzled by the colours
For Jesus to be seen?

If he stood amongst us
Would we treat him just the same,
And argue in two thousand years
Just who it was to blame?

Or has he come and gone again,
And did nobody care?
Perhaps he found a second cross
Was just too much to bear.

Peter Kuck

DESIRES FOR PEACE

In my dreams, I see
No more wars between countries,
No more starvation in this world,
No more earthquakes devastating countries,
No more volcanic or terrorist explosions,
No more refugees in this world,
No more suffering and tragedy in this world.
My desires for the future are,
Everyone to respect different colours, shapes and sizes,
Everyone to have the freedom to live,
Everyone to be proud of their own identity,
Everyone having the same amount of love,
Everyone having love for one another,
Everyone to put their colour, race, religion together
To build up one single community
But most of all I want,
Everyone to live a life according to the values
Of love, peace and truth
And to remember and be thankful for all
The beauty in this precious world.

Mahmooda Begum Ali (15)

Peace For The Future?

The television shows pictures of another battlefield
Horrific scenes that sadly shock no more
What is the reason for this senseless destruction:
Is it merely greed, or an unquenchable thirst for power?

These images burn into our memories
We feel helpless not knowing how to intervene
Each succeeding battle brings greater tragedy
With innocent people caught in the juggernaut's path.

We read newspapers, watch television
And debate the actions we think our representatives ought to take
When they meet to ponder our futures
Over hors-d'oeuvres in Brussels.

It's easy to say that terrible things like this shouldn't happen
To shake your head and refuse to get involved.
But change will only come when we stand up to be counted
Stopping petty dictators in their tracks.

For if we sit back and do absolutely nothing
Refusing to acknowledge the troubles ahead
Today's nightmare will become tomorrow's news
And the listlessness of despair will be all we have left to share.

Mavis Simpson

TRAVELLING

Movement is clear and nice,
adding for life, so much spice
going places all world over,
far beyond Rockies, maybe from Dover.

For all and sundry, a heavenly feast
much to gain, from it not the least
refreshment, recuperation, no sentiment,
all seasons, particularly Christmastime to Lent.

Often this sort of period
covers year, even a lesser myriad,
you cannot claim rolling stone
gathers moss onto another clone.

Sure thing travel, is much of a blessing
for patient revival, alternate dressing.
Renew acquaintances, meet up friend,
pack those bags, and follow the trend.

High or low, people indulge it,
never look back, no need to fit.
All persons climb to change or design,
meaning intently follow that line.

Of joining boat, plane or bus,
no running, no danger, or fuss.
Today everyone's joy of living,
so much on offer, loaded lots giving.

So take some choice,
maybe not Rolls Royce.
Hobson's is no alternative,
for life's 'Cling, clang' live . . .

So . . . go . . . go

N Lemel

FRIENDSHIP

Friendship is loving and giving,
Friendship is caring and needing
Friendship is understanding and knowing,
When each one drifts off a known path,
Then keep the pathway narrow and clear
From suffering and pain,
Then friendship will always keep drawing
Those near and dear.

Anne McTavish

PEACE IN OUR TIME

Over the centuries, time after time,
Wars have erupted in every clime.
Nations searching for new lands to invade
Hoping to have more scope for their trade.
History is full of battles and strife,
Throughout the ages warfare was rife.
From the primitive spear to the atomic war,
Guns and bombs have been used more and more.
It is hoped that with progress all wars will end,
And little by little, peace will descend.
God's peace for all times and in every way
Please God let us see it before long we pray.

Jean C Pease

DESIRE FOR PEACE

Our past as bloody as the rest
and like others, thought it was right
to conquer all, taking the best,
leaving only their will to fight.

No country has a right to own
another whatever reason,
but help them when they stand alone,
when nature strikes with every season.

With so much sorrow in each land,
some are rich, while others are poor,
show you care and give them a hand,
thankful when they open their door.

Common people want lasting peace,
an end to wars, present or past,
enjoy their lives when hate will cease,
breathe a sigh of relief at last.

A Odger

LIFT UP YOUR HEARTS

Raise your heart, and whisper a prayer.
Clasping hands, think Christ is always there.
Fill your mind, with pure loving care
Lord help us, Lord let us share
The trials of the world today
Lord help us, that the trials will fade away
Concentrate daily, in silent prayer
Bringing a feeling of peace everywhere
A feeling of calmness in the air.
Loving arms around you in His presence
Stretching arms, that surround our prayer.
On bended knee, our hearts aflame
Filled with love, from the Lord above
When we kneel and bow our head in prayer
Knowing Christ will be always there
Raise your heart, and whisper a prayer
For a lovely world, just outside there
A prayer for peace, that crimes will cease
A prayer for harmony, a prayer of love
On clouds of heaven, to our Lord above
'I give you peace, my peace I give you'
Precious spoken words, so good and true.
To raise our saddened hearts
With love anew
Grant our prayer, please we implore,
To Christ our Lord, whom we adore.

Blanche Naughton

TRANQUIL TALK

Soaring above the stricken lands at war,
like pristine, pure white, ivory doves,
our dreams survive abominable uproar;
their sails, sunlit, undiminished loves.
Whilst dictators underlings' rights abuse,
like rapacious crows rampant for meat,
overthrowing methods that the righteous use,
so the visionary's ideals stay sweet.
Beauty with which Bible stays the course,
leaps ahead like lightning in a storm,
permeates belligerent with force
of spirit ethereal and warm.
God's music, his artistic ways deny
the supremacy of hell on earth
and honeyed harmony fells battle cry,
contorts kill with our Almighty's worth.
Peace for posterity's thematic pledge
of pious opposed to conflict lust;
tip-toeing in gold we poise at the edge
of despair, not relinquishing trust;
out of the havoc aggressor must wreak,
in the stillness of night when we're praying,
the voices of reason silently speak,
contretemps of destruction delaying.
Way back in history, wielding his sword
the insensitive upstart began
his crusade of contempt, hate for the Lord,
peace still ultimate saviour of man.

Ruth Daviat

THE EMPTY BOWLS

Oh! Rich man, listen to the gospels,
if you can help us when we cry!
We are your coloured brothers,
be that good Samaritan! Do not pass me by!

Another soul has passed away today!
Hear us when we call, hear us when we cry!
It could be you! Alas 'tis I!
I am hungry, you are fed, my whole family they are dead!

I am all alone, a little boy entwined,
send me food! Send me love! Let it be in time.
My father! My mother! God rest their weary souls,
we laid them down to rest today in those dry clay holes!

How can this world just leave us to travel all alone!
Money! Be their God, their hearts are made of stone!
We are brave in spirit! Our seeds are scattered, sown.

J J Mattsea

WHITE DOVE

White dove of peace
I see your wings
As you float across the sky
You to me are many things
The softness of a baby's cheek
In innocence at its birth
Lying within a mother's arms
So peaceful on this earth
Where does all violence begin
Surely not in the womb
We care so much for our unborn
Their birth cannot be too soon
It does not matter what our colour
We all have needs, want love
Food to nurture, help us grow
Sun, moon and stars, raindrops from above
God gave us all a beginning
A start along life's way
The purpose in our being is
Learn to share each and every day
If all mothers on this earth would say
You cannot have our sons
Could we then have war and violence
No place would there be for guns
We have so much to give one another
Where does all conflict arise
It is in greed for money
Possessions are never a prize
Man should not want to kill his brother
Look at the tears in a mother's eyes.

Elizabeth Cowley-Guscott

Cold

I flick through today's paper.
Refugees are fleeing from their homes,
Whilst their countries are ripped apart.
Political prisoners across the world
Are trapped by their beliefs.
People are bought and sold as slaves.
Continents are torn,
And millions are in poverty's heartless grip.

In nations of peace, hooligans and vandals
Destroy their country's pride
People and pride are sold,
For material gain.
Many are homeless,
And are left alone to freeze or die -
Whatever, as long as they don't bother anyone.
Gangs fight over the streets
Which have become mini war zones,
Innocent people dare not step out
After dark.

Despite these horrors we see and read of,
Few try to help, few even care,
The rich get richer,
The poor get poorer.
The divide widens,
And humans become increasingly cold.

Jordan Steer

THE TRAUMA OF WAR

Violence displayed in the woes of war
Bitter conflict that some deplore
To boast of the number of killings scored
Causing the suffering of bloodshed and gore

Such examples us adults set, for the error of our ways
'Star Wars' battles in space age displays
Has nothing been learnt from our TV screens
Tears of trauma, war's consequence screams.

R Humphrey

Abused Symbol

A dove sat in a sunbeam
Piercing through the narrow streets.
A shot, two feathers twisted
Caught in currents of hate,
Their whiteness red spotted.
Shocked the dove flew to the woods -
Who in that familiar town
Would act like this?

Above a makeshift shelter
A dove coo-ed in a tree . . .
Its throat swelled as it tried
To soothe the crying of a frightened hungry child.
Frantically the mother rocked it;
A feather dropped from the spread ruff.
The child looked, tried to catch it,
For a fleeting moment forgot its pain.

An imagined insult
Flared the feud from the past.
Every generation there involved,
Even the women were drawn in.
Furtive movements across the valley,
Volleys of shots, but nothing gained,
Just a white fluttering in No Man's Land
Where the dove of peace lay mortally wounded

Pure gentle symbol, so abused
Still devotedly trying however bruised.

Di Bagshawe

INFORMATION

We hope you have enjoyed reading this book - and that you will continue to enjoy it in the coming years.

If you like reading and writing poetry drop us a line, or give us a call, and we'll send you a free information pack.

Write to :-
**Triumph House Information
Remus House
Coltsfoot Drive
Peterborough
PE2 9JX
(01733) 898102**